WHO'S AFRAID OF VIRGINIA WOOLF?

NOTES

including
- *Life and Background*
- *Edward Albee and the Theater of the Absurd*
- *The Stage Setting*
- *The Meaning of the Title*
- *List of Characters*
- *Analysis of the Drama*
- *The Significance of the Titles of the Acts*
- *Character Analyses*
- *Review Questions*
- *Selected Bibliography*

by
Cynthia C. McGowan, M.A.
University of Nebraska
and
James L. Roberts, Ph.D.
Professor of English
University of Nebraska

D0465726

INCORPORATED

LINCOLN, NEBRASKA 68501

Editor

Gary Carey, M.A.
University of Colorado

Consulting Editor

James L. Roberts, Ph.D.
Department of English
University of Nebraska

Cliffs Notes, Inc.   Lincoln, Nebraska

CONTENTS

LIFE AND BACKGROUND

There has been no official biography of Edward Albee and, therefore, such knowledge as is available to the reader might be subject to some distortions of fact. Edward Albee was born on March 12, 1928, in Washington, D.C. At the present time, his biological parentage is not public. He was adopted by very wealthy parents when he was two weeks old, and he carries the name of his adopted grandfather, Edward Franklin Albee, who was, among other things, part owner of a chain of theaters. This fact, however, seemingly has little relation to Albee's later theatrical career even though, as a child, Albee often found himself in the presence of prominent theater people.

Albee showed an interest in creative endeavors very early in life. His first attempts were with poetry, and by the time he was twelve, he had written his first play, a three-act farce called *Aliqueen*. Since his wealthy parents summered and wintered in different places, Albee's education was, to say the least, erratic. He was dismissed from one prep school (Lawrenceville School) when he was fifteen, was sent to Valley Forge Military Academy, and subsequently dismissed from there and graduated from Choate School. While at the latter, he submitted and had his first poem published in a Texas literary magazine *(Kaleidoscope)* and also his first one-act play was published in the *Choate Literary Magazine*.

While in Trinity College briefly, he became familiar with another side of the theater when he acted in a Maxwell Anderson play. Leaving college in 1947, Albee moved to Greenwich Village, N. Y., and occupied himself with a variety of odd jobs even though he was reportedly the weekly recipient of a trust fund. He shared an apartment with a composer and through him met many people in the music world. He also wrote for a radio station. His other odd jobs included being a waiter, bartender, salesman, and a Western Union delivery messenger.

In 1958, just before his thirtieth birthday, Albee finished *The Zoo Story*, the long one-act drama that would launch him on his career. After sending it to various theatrical producers in New York, a friend sent it to an acquaintance in Europe and it was finally produced in Berlin on September 28, 1959. After being a success there and being staged in numerous other cities in Germany, it was then presented in New York at the Off-Broadway Provincetown Play-house in 1960. Albee attracted quite a bit of critical success with this play but not much popular success. Then in 1962, he achieved both critical and popular success with *Who's Afraid of Virginia Woolf?*. The play won the coveted New York Drama Critics Award and every other major award except the Pulitzer Prize, and it was made into a very successful motion picture with slight, but some-times important, changes from the dramatic script.

Although Albee has continued to write significant drama *(A Delicate Balance* in 1966 won the Pulitzer Prize), none of his later plays have won the critical and popular acclaim awarded to *Who's Afraid of Virginia Woolf?*

EDWARD ALBEE AND THE THEATER OF THE ABSURD

Even though Albee's *Who's Afraid of Virginia Woolf* would not be strictly classified as belonging to the movement known as "The Theater of the Absurd," there are, however, a great many elements of this play which are closely aligned with or which grew out of the dramas which are classified as being a part of "The Theater of the Absurd." Furthermore, the movement emerged on the literary scene just prior to and during the beginning of Albee's formative, creative years. Also, his early plays — *The Zoo Story, The American Dream,* and *Sand Box* — which will be discussed later, do belong rather directly with the Absurdist movement and they employ most of the themes, motifs, ideas, and techniques found in the plays of "The Theater of the Absurd." Furthermore, *Who's Afraid of Virginia Woolf* also utilizes many of the techniques and ideas of his earlier plays — for example the lost or non-existent child is a con-stant factor in many of Albee's plays of all periods. Consequently, in its simplest terms, Albee's early short dramas are essential studies to *Who's Afraid of Virginia Woolf,* his first full length drama. In addition to a knowledge of Albee's own early plays, an understand-ing of the entire movement of "The Theater of the Absurd" and the relationship of Albee's early plays to that movement will, in part, illuminate aspects of *Who's Afraid of Virginia Woolf.*

To begin, even though the movement known as "The Theater of the Absurd" was not a consciously conceived movement, and it has never had any clear cut philosophical doctrines, no organized attempt to win converts, and no meetings, it has characteristics which set it apart from other experiments in drama. Each of the main playwrights of the movement seemed to have developed independently of the other. The playwrights most often connected with the movement are Samuel Beckett, Eugene Ionesco, Jean Genet, and Arthur Adamov. The early plays of Edward Albee and Harold Pinter fit into this classification but they have also written plays that move far away from the Theater of the Absurd.

In viewing the plays that comprise this movement, we must forsake the theater of coherently developed situations, we must forsake characterizations that are rooted in the logic of motivation and reaction, we must forget (sometimes) settings that bear an intrinsic, realistic or obvious relationship in the drama as a whole, we must forget the use of language as a tool of logical communication, and we must forget cause and effect relationships found in traditional drama. By their use of a number of puzzling devices, these playwrights have gradually accustomed audiences to a new kind of relationship between theme and presentation. In these seemingly queer and fantastic plays, the external world is often depicted as menacing, devouring and unknown; the settings and situations often make us vaguely uncomfortable; the world itself seems incoherent and frightening and strange, but at the same time, hauntingly poetic and familiar.

These are some of the reasons which prompt the critic to classify them under the heading "Theater of the Absurd" — a title which comes not from a dictionary definition of the world "absurd," but rather from Martin Esslin's book *The Theatre of the Absurd*, in which he maintains that these dramatists write from a "sense of metaphysical anguish at the absurdity of the human condition." But other writers such as Kafka, Camus, and Sartre have argued from the same philosophical position. The essential difference is that critics like Camus have presented their arguments in a highly formal discourse with logical and precise views which prove their thesis within the framework of traditional forms. On the contrary, the Theater of the Absurd seeks to wed form and content into an indissoluble whole, so as to gain a further unity of meaning and impact. This theater has, as Esslin has pointed out, "renounced arguing *about* the absurdity of the human condition; it merely presents it in being — that is, in terms of concrete stage images of the absurdity of existence."

Too often, however, the viewer is tempted to note these basic similarities (and others to be later noted) and to dismiss an individual playwright as merely another absurdist writer. Also, too often, the critic fails to note the distinctive differences in each dramatist. Since these writers (dramatists) do not belong to any deliberate or conscious movement, they should be evaluated for their individual concerns as well as their contributions to the total concept of the Theater of the Absurd. In fact, most of these playwrights consider themselves to be lonely rebels and outsiders, isolated in their own private world. As noted above, there have been no manifestos, no theses, no conferences and no collaborations. Each has developed along his own unique line; each in his own way is individually and distinctly different. Therefore it is important to see how Ionesco both belongs to the Theater of the Absurd and equally important, how he differs from the other writers. First let us note a few of the basic differences.

The Differences:

One of Samuel Beckett's main concerns is with the polarity of existence. In *Waiting for Godot, Endgame,* and *Krapp's Last Tape,* we have such characteristic polarities as sight versus blindness, life — death, time present — time past, body — intellect, waiting — not waiting, going — not going, and *literally* dozens more. Beckett's main concern, then, seems to be to place man and characterize man's existence in terms of these polarities. To do this, Beckett groups his characters in pairs, i.e., we have Vladimir and Estragon, or Didi and Gogo, Hamm and Clov, Pozzo and Lucky, Nagg and Nell, and Krapp's present voice and past voice. Essentially, however, Beckett's characters remain a puzzle which each individual viewer must solve.

In contrast to Beckett, Eugene Ionesco's characters are seen in terms of singularity. Whereas Beckett's characters stand in pairs *outside* of society but converse with each other, Ionesco's characters are placed in the midst of society, but they stand alone in an alien world with no personal identity and no one to whom they can communicate. For example, the characters in *The Bald Soprano* are *in* society, but scream meaningless phrases at each other and there is no communication. And whereas Beckett's plays take place on strange and alien landscapes (some of his plays remind one of a world already transformed by some holocaust or created by some surrealist) Ionesco's plays are set against the most traditional elements in our society—the standard English drawing room in *The Bald Soprano*, a typical street scene in *Rhinoceros*, an average study in *The Lesson*, etc.

The language of the two playwrights also differs greatly. Beckett's dialogue recalls the disjointed phantasmagoria of a dream world; Ionesco's language is rooted in the banalities, cliches and platitudes of everyday speech; Beckett uses language to show man isolated in a world and unable to communicate because language is a barrier to communication. Ionesco, on the other hand, uses language to show the failure of communication because there is nothing to say; thus in *The Bald Soprano*, and other plays, the dialogue is filled with cliches and banalities.

In contrast to the basic sympathy we feel for both Beckett's and Ionesco's characters, especially characters like Berenger, Jean Genet's characters almost revile the audience from the moment that they appear on the stage. His theme is more openly stated. He is concerned with the hatred which exists in the world. In *The Maids*, each maid hates not just her employer and not just her own sister, but also her own self. Therefore, she plays the other roles so as to exhaust her own hatred of herself against herself. Basically, then, there is a great sense of repugnance in Genet's characters. This revulsion derives partially from the fact that Genet's interest, so different from Beckett's and Ionesco's, is in the psychological exploration of man's predilection to being trapped in his own egocentric world rather than facing the realities of existence. Man for Genet is trapped by his own fantastic illusions. Man's absurdity results partially from the fact that he prefers his own disjointed images to those of reality. Thus, in Genet's direction for the production of *The Blacks*, he writes that the play should never be played before a totally black audience. If there are no white people present, then one of the Negroes in the audience must wear a white mask; if the Negro refuses, then a white mannequin must be used and the actors must play the drama for this mannequin. Thus there must be a white audience, someone for the Negroes to revile. Since a Negro audience by its color would recognize and prefer the identical images that the actors are creating, there must be the white person to note the distortion of reality.

In contrast to Ionesco, Arthur Adamov, in his themes, is more closely aligned to the Kafkaesque of the existentialist school, but his technique is that of the theater of the absurd. His interest is in establishing some proof that the individual does exist, and he shows how man becomes more alienated from his fellow man as he attempts to establish his own personal identity. For example, in *Professor Tarrane*, the central character, hoping to prove his innocence of a certain accusation, actually convicts himself through his own defense. For Adamov, man attempting to prove his own existence actually proves that he does not exist. Language, therefore, for Adamov serves as an inadequate system of communication and actually in some cases serves to the detriment of man, since by language and man's use of language, man often finds himself trapped in the circumstances he previously hoped to avoid. Ultimately, Adamov's characters fail to communicate because each is interested only in his own egocentric self. Each character propounds his own troubles and his own achievements, but the words reverberate as against a stone wall. They are heard only by the audience. Adamov's plays are often grounded in the dream-world atmosphere; and while they are presenting a series of outwardly confusing scenes of almost hallucinatory quality, they, at the same time, attack or denounce the confusion present in modern man.

Characteristic of all these writers is a notable absence of any excess concern over sex. Edward Albee, an American, differs significantly in his emphasis and concern with the sexual substructure of society. The overtones of homosexuality in *The Zoo Story* are carried further until the young man in *The American Dream* becomes the incarnation of the muscular and ideally handsome young homosexual who, since he has no inner feelings, passively allows anyone "to take pleasure from my groin." In *The Sandbox*, the angel of death is again seen as the muscle-bound young homosexual who spends his time scantily dressed and performing calisthenics on a beach while preparing for a career in Hollywood.

Similarities:

Although all of the writers have varying concerns, they also have much in common, because their works reflect a moral and philosophical climate in which most of our civilization finds itself today. Again, as noted above, even though there were no manifestos, no organized movements, there are still certain concerns that are basic to all of the writers and Ionesco's works are concerned with these basic ideas or concerns.

Beyond the technical and strange illusionary techniques which prompt the critic to group these plays into a category, there are larger and ultimately, more significant concerns by which each dramatist, in spite of his differences, is akin to the other. Aside from such similarities as violation of traditional beginning, middle, and end (or exposition, complication, and denouement) or the refusal to tell a straight-forward connected story with a nice plot, the disappearance of traditional dramatic forms and techniques, they are also concerned over the failure of communication in modern society which leaves man alienated, and they are concerned over a lack of individuality or an over-emphasis on conformity in our society. They use time and place to imply important ideas, and finally they reject traditional logic for a type of nonlogic which ultimately implies something about the nature of the universe. Implicit in many of these concerns is an attack on a society or world which possesses no set standards of values or behavior.

First, let's examine the concern over the lack of communication. In Edward Albee's plays, each character is existing in his own private ego. Each makes a futile attempt to get another character to understand him, but as the attempt is contrived, there is more alienation. Thus, finally, because of a lack of communication, Peter, the conformist in *The Zoo Story*, is provoked into killing Jerry, the individualist; or in *The Sandbox*, a continuation of *The American Dream*, Mommy and Daddy bury Grandma because she talks incessantly but says nothing significant. The irony is that Grandma is the only character who does say anything significant, but Mommy and Daddy, the people who discard her, are incapable of understanding her.

But in Ionesco's plays, this failure of communication leads often to even more drastic results. Like Albee's *Zoo Story*, the professor in *The Lesson* must kill the student partly because she doesn't understand his communication. Or Berenger, in *The Killers*, has uttered so many cliches that by the end of the play, he has even convinced himself that the killers should kill him. In *The Chairs*, the old people, needing to express their thoughts, address themselves to a mass of empty chairs which, as the play progresses, crowd all else off the stage. In *Maid to Marry*, communication is so bad that the maid, when she appears on the stage, turns out to be a rather homely man. And ultimately, in Ionesco's *Rhinoceros*, the inability to communicate causes an entire race of so-called rational human beings to be metamorphosed into a herd of rhinoceroses thereby abandoning all hopes of language as a means of communication.

In Adamov's *Professor Taranne*, the professor, in spite of all his desperate attempts, is unable to get people to acknowledge his identity because there is no communication. Likewise, Pinter's plays show individuals grouped on the stage, but each person fails to achieve any degree of effective communication. The concern with communication is carried to its illogical extreme in two works: in Genet's *The Blacks*, one character says "We shall even have the decency—a decency learned from you—to make communication impossible." And in another, Beckett's *Act Without Words*, we have our first play in this movement to use absolutely no dialogue. And even without dialogue, all the action on the stage suggests the inability of man to communicate.

Beckett's characters are tied together by a fear of being left entirely alone and they therefore cling to that last hope of establishing some communication with another. His plays give the impression of man totally lost in a disintegrating society, or as in *Endgame*, of man alone after society has already disintegrated. In *Waiting for Godot*, the two derelicts are seen conversing in repetitive, strangely fragmented dialogue that possesses an illusory, haunting effect, while they are waiting for Godot, a vague, never-defined being who will bring them some communication about—what? Salvation? Death? A reason for living? The impetus for dying? No one knows and the safest thing to say is that the two are waiting for someone (something) which will give them the impetus to continue living and waiting or something which will give them meaning and direction to life. And as Beckett clearly demonstrates, those who rush hither and yon in search of meanings find it no quicker than those who sit and wait. But everyone leaves the theater with the realization that these tramps are strangely tied to one another; and yet, even though they bicker and fight, and even though they have exhausted all conversation—notice that the second act is repetitive and almost identical—the loneliness and weakness in each calls out to the others, and they are held by a mystical bond of interdependence. But in spite of this strange dependency, neither is able to communicate with the other. The other two characters, Pozzo and Lucky, are on a journey without any apparent goal, and are symbolically tied together. One talks, the other says nothing. The waiting of Vladimir and Estragon and the journeying of Pozzo and Lucky offer themselves as contrasts to various activities in the modern world each leading to no fruitful end;

therefore, each pair is hopelessly alienated from the other pair. For example, when Pozzo falls and yells for help, Vladimir and Estragon continue their talk, but throughout their dialogue nothing is communicated; all is hopeless or as Vladimir aphoristically replies to one of Estragon's long discourses, "We are all born mad. Some remain so." In their attempts at conversation and communication, these two tramps have a fastidious correctness and a grave propriety that suggest that they could be socially accepted; but their fastidiousness and propriety are inordinately comic when contrasted with their ragged appearance.

Their fumbling ineffectuality in their attempts at conversation seems to represent the ineptness of all mankind in its attempt at communication. And it rapidly becomes apparent that Vladimir and Estragon, as representatives of modern man, cannot formulate any cogent or useful play of action; and what is more pathetic, they cannot communicate their helpless longings to one another. While failing to possess enough individualism to go their separate ways, they nevertheless are different enough to embrace most of our society. In the final analysis, their one positive gesture lies in their strength to wait. And man is terribly alone in his waiting. Ionesco shows the same ideas in the end of *Rhinoceros* when we see Berenger totally alone as a result partly of a failure in communication.

Each dramatist has, therefore, presented a critique of modern society by showing the total collapse of communication. The technique used is that of evolving a theme about communication by presenting a series of seemingly disjointed speeches. The accumulative effect of these speeches is a devastating commentary on the failure of communication in modern society.

In conjunction with the general attack on communication, the second aspect common to the dramatists is the lack of individuality encountered in modern civilization. Generally, the point seems to be that man does not know himself. He has lost all sense of individualism and either functions isolated and alien or else finds himself lost amid repetition and conformity.

Jean Genet's play, *The Maids*, opens with the maid Claire playing the role of her employer while her sister Solange plays the role of Claire. Therefore, we have Claire calling or referring to Solange as Claire. By the time the audience realizes that the two sisters are imitating someone else, each character has lost her individualism; therefore, as Claire later portrays Solange, who portrays the employer, and vice versa, we gradually realize that part of Genet's intent was to illustrate the total lack of individuality and furthermore, to show that each character becomes vibrantly alive only when functioning in the image of another personality.

Other dramatists present their attack on society's destruction of individualism by different means, but the attack still has the same thematic intent. In Albee's *The American Dream*, Mommy and Daddy are obviously generic names for any mommy and daddy. Albee is not concerned with individualizing his characters. They remain types and as types are seen at times in terms of extreme burlesque. So, unlike Beckett's tramps, and more like Ionesco's characters, Albee's people are seen as Babbitt-like caricatures and satires on the "American Dream" type, and the characters remain mannequins with no delineations. Thus in Ionesco's *The Bald Soprano,* the Martins can assume the roles of the Smiths and begin the play over because there is no distinction between the two sets of characters.

As emphasized elsewhere in this volume, Ionesco has written most extensively about the failure of individualism most effectively in his most famous play, *Rhinoceros.* To repeat, in this play, our society today has emphasized conformity to such an extent and has rejected individualism so completely that Ionesco demonstrates with inverse logic how stupid it is not to conform with all society and be metamorphosed into a rhinoceros. This play aptly illustrates how two concerns of the absurdists — lack of communication and the lack of individualism — are combined, each to support the other. Much of Ionesco's dialogue in this play seems to be the distilled essence of the commonplace. One cliche follows another. We are further startled because this dialogue is spoken within the framework of a wildly improbable situation. In a typically common street with the typical common cliches about weather and work being uttered, the morning calm is shattered by a rhinoceros as it charges through the streets. Then two rhinoceroses, then more. Ridiculous arguments then develop as to whether they are African or Asiatic rhinoceroses. We soon learn that there is an epidemic of metamorphoses; all are changing into rhinoceroses. Soon only three individuals are left. Then in the face of this absurd situation, we have the equally appalling justifications and reasons in favor of being metamorphosed advocated in such cliches as "We must join the crowd." "We must move with the times," "We've got to build our life on new foundations," etc. Suddenly it almost seems foolish not to become a rhinoceros. In the end, Berenger's sweetheart, Daisy, succumbs to the pressure of society, relinquishes her individualism, and joins the society of rhinoceroses — not because she wants to, but rather because she is afraid not to. She cannot revolt against society even to remain a human being. Berenger is left alone totally isolated, with his individualism. And what good is his humanity in a world of rhinoceroses?

At first glance it would seem obvious that Ionesco wishes to indicate the triumph of the individual, who, although caught in a society that has gone mad, refuses to surrender his sense of identity. But if we look more closely, we see that Ionesco has no intention of leaving us on this hopeful and comforting note.

In his last speech, Berenger makes it clear that his stand is rendered absurd. What does his humanity avail him in a world of beasts? Finally, he wishes that he also had changed, only now he realizes that it is too late. All he can do is feebly reassert his joy in being human. His statement carries little conviction. Thus Ionesco has dealt with the haunting theme of the basic meaning and value of personal identity in relationship to society. If one depends entirely upon the society in which one lives for a sense of reality and identity, it is impossible to take a stand against that society without reducing oneself to nothingness in the process. Berenger instinctively felt repelled by the tyranny that had sprung up around him, but he had no sense of identity that would have enabled him to combat this evil with anything resembling a positive force. Probably any action he could have taken would have led to eventual defeat, but defeat would have been infinitely preferable to the limbo in which he is finally consigned. Thus, Ionesco has masterfully joined two themes: the lack of individualism and the failure of communication. But unlike Beckett who handles the same themes by presenting his characters as derelicts and outcasts from society, Ionesco's treatment seems even more devastating for having placed them in the very middle of the society from which they are estranged.

Ultimately, the absurdity of man's condition is partially a result of his being compelled to exist without his individualism and in a society which does not possess any degree of effective communication. Essentially, therefore, the theater of the absurd is not a positive drama. It does not try to prove that man is in a meaningless world as did Camus or Sartre: it does not offer any solutions: instead, it demonstrates the absurdity and illogicality of the world we live in. Nothing is ever settled; there are no positive statements; no conclusions are ever reached and, what few actions there are have no meaning, particularly in relation to the action. That is, one action carries no more significance than does its opposite action. For example, the man tying his shoe in *The Bald Soprano* — a common event — is magnified into a fantastic act while the appearance of rhinoceroses in the middle of a calm afternoon is not at all memorable and evokes only the most trite and insignificant remarks. Also, Pozzo and Lucky's frantic running and searching are no more important than Vladimir and Estragon's sitting and waiting. And Genet presents his Blacks as outcasts from and misfits in society but refrains from making any positive statement regarding the Black person's role in our society — the question of whether society is to be integrated or segregated is to Genet a matter of perfect indifference. It would still be society and the individual would still be outside it.

No conclusions or resolutions can ever be offered because these plays are essentially circular and repetitive in nature. *The Bald Soprano* begins over again with a new set of characters, and other plays end at the same point at which they began, thus obviating any possible conclusions or positive statements. *The American Dream* ends with the coming of a second child, this time one that is fully grown and the twin to the other child who had years before entered the family as a baby and upset the static condition; thus, thematically, the play ends as it began. Therefore, in all of these playwrights and dramas, the sense of repetition, the circular structure, the static quality, the lack of cause and effect, and the lack of apparent progression all suggest the sterility and lack of values in the modern world.

Early critics referred to the *Theater of the Absurd* as a theater in transition, meaning that it was to lead to something different. So far this has not happened and moreover it is rapidly becoming accepted as a distinct genre in its own right. The themes utilized by these dramatists are not new; thus, the success of the plays must often depend upon the effectiveness of the technique and the new ways by which the dramatists illustrate their themes. But the techniques are still so new that many people are confused by a production of one of these plays. But more important, if the technique serves to emphasize the absurdity of man's position in the universe, then to present this concept by a series of ridiculous situations is only to render man's position more absurd; and in actuality, the techniques then reinforce that condition which the dramatists bewail. In other words, to present the failure of communication by a series of disjointed and seemingly incoherent utterances lends itself to the accusation that functionalism is carried to a ridiculous extreme. But this is what the absurdist wanted to do. He was tired of logical discourses pointing out step by step the absurdity of the universe: he began with the philosophical premise that the universe is absurd, and then created plays which illustrated conclusively that the universe is indeed absurd and that perhaps this play is an additional absurdity.

In conclusion, if the public can accept these unusual uses of technique to support thematic concerns, then do we have plays which present, dramatically, powerful and vivid views on the absurdity of the human condition—an absurdity which is the result of society's destruction of individualism, of the failure of communication, of being forced to conform to a world of mediocrity, where no action is meaningful? And as the tragic outcasts of these plays are presented in terms of Burlesque, man is reminded that his position and that of human existence in general is essentially absurd. Every play in the Theater of the Absurd mirrors the chaos and basic disorientation of modern man. Each laughs in anguish at the confusion that exists in contemporary society; hence, all share a basic point of view, while varying widely in scope and structure.

THE SETTING

The setting of the drama is in a university town which in itself gives a special aura to the play. The characters in the drama represent the types of people who have been given the most disciplined training in the best that has been thought and said throughout the history of civilization. Consequently, we are exposed to several very civilized people acting in a way that is at times uncivilized and barbaric.

The name of the town that George and Martha live in is called New Carthage. Carthage is the name of the ancient classical city which was the site of the great love story of Dido and Aeneas and was ultimately destroyed because it was a city of "unholy loves," as St. Augustine referred to it.

The stage setting itself is also significant. Even though the script does not call for it, George and Martha's living room (the only set for the play) usually has a picture of George and Martha Washington displayed somewhere in clear view of the audience. In addition, there is traditionally an American flag on a stand (or otherwise displayed) and/or an American eagle or coat of arms prominently displayed somewhere.

THE TITLE

On the most basic level, the title is the substitution of the name of the famous British novelist Virginia Woolf for the name of the Big Bad Wolf of the nursery rhyme. The obvious correlation is the homophonic relationship of the last names—Woolf and Wolf. The hilarity which the substitution causes can be accounted for most directly as the result of the drunkenness of the guest who, in a drunken stupor, finds the intellectualizing of a nursery rhyme to be unaccountably comic. The use of the nursery rhyme, however, becomes central to the "fun and games" which characterize so much of the drama.

Other than the obvious similarity of the last names, the title seems to make an oblique comment on the drama itself. In the nursery rhyme which deals with fear of the unknown or possible evil in the person of the big bad wolf, the first two pigs ignore the possibility of the evil of the wolf and, as a result, are destroyed. The third little pig, recognizing the danger of the wolf, makes provisions against destruction and consequently survives.

Characters in the novels of Virginia Woolf can often be characterized as being apprehensive about, if not terrified of, life, and, like the first two little pigs, fail to make (or are unable to make) the proper provisions to cope with life. Virginia Woolf's own life was characterized by periods of madness, and so it is not surprising that she should deal in her novels with the intolerability of life and subsequent madness. The reference, then, to Virginia Woolf could function as a portent because George and Martha are playing a dangerous game which could drive either or both of them into madness since both of their lives are intolerable.

LIST OF CHARACTERS

GEORGE

A forty-six-year-old professor of history in a small New England college who is married to the daughter of the president of the college.

MARTHA

George's fifty-two-year-old wife, a domineering, discontented woman who alternately loves and reviles her husband.

NICK

A new arrival on the faculty who is about thirty years old and interested in getting ahead.

HONEY

Nick's wife, a rather uninteresting woman whose relationship with Nick and fear of adult responsibility have kept her a child.

CRITICAL ANALYSIS

FUN AND GAMES

ACT I: Scene i

Since *Who's Afraid of Virginia Woolf* is a very long play with each act being rather lengthy, for the sake of critical discussion and explication, each act will be divided into scenes even though this was not done in the original play. The scenic division will follow the classic method of scene division; that is, there is a new scene with either the entrance or exit of a character from the stage. Thus, scene i comprises the entrance of George and Martha and ends with the entrance of Honey and Nick.

While the language of the play might be acceptable today, in 1962 the opening language was startling, if not shocking, to the audience. The play opens with George and Martha returning home from a party at her father's house. There is a loud crash followed by Martha variously swearing, cursing, shouting ("braying" as George calls it) and insulting her husband, George. (She calls him a "cluck" and a "dumbbell" and insults him continually in other ways.) As she looks about her home, she is reminded of a line from a Bette Davis film, and the line, "What a dump," delivered in imitation of Bette Davis, has since become one of the most famous lines from the play. The movie character that Martha is quoting is "discontent," and the scene shows that Martha is also discontent with her house, with her husband who never does anything ("You never do anything; you never *mix.* . . ."), and most importantly with her own life. Her discontentment is important because this will be one of the reasons that the couple has created the imaginary child.

Since it is 2 A.M. and neither of them is sober, George assumes that since they are home, one small nightcap would be alright, but suddenly Martha springs the news on him that company is coming. Martha's main justification for having invited guests over is that her "daddy," who is the President of the college where George teaches, told her to be "nice" to this new couple. Martha's repetition three times about her father's instructions suggests already that her "daddy" has an influence on George and Martha's lives that will figure significantly in later scenes.

After Martha informs him who the couple is, George tells Martha that he wishes "you'd stop *springing* things on me all the time . . . you're always *springing* things on me." Beginning with this statement, we see that part of the play will deal with the concept of who is running or managing their life style. During the first part of the drama, Martha seems to be in almost complete control of their lives, but a change will later occur and it will be George who will *spring* things on Martha.

Martha reminds George of the nursery rhyme that apparently was sung at the party at her father's house. Someone had substituted the name of the famous British novelist Virginia Woolf for the Big Bad Wolf. The mention of this nursery rhyme with its intellectual variation characterizes much of the first act with its fun and games, with the shifting from intellectual conversation to baby talk and to talk of babies (see note on the title in the preceding section).

The rest of the scene shows the extreme variance in the relationship between the two. When George fails to respond to the song, Martha will first tell him "You make me puke" and then will follow this insult by their both laughing, and her requesting more ice in her drink and wanting a "great big sloppy kiss" from George. Thus, their relationship moves from one of grand insults to one of open sexuality. We are now prepared to see both react on a variety of levels. Martha's age is also emphasized in this scene since she is six years older than George. This implies that she is, as she later says, the earth mother capable of controlling both George and men much younger than she is.

When the doorbell rings, she *orders* George to answer it. She forces George into the role of "houseboy" as she will later force Nick to answer the bell after he has been a failure in bed. But before George answers the doorbell, he warns Martha three times not to start in "on the bit about the kid." This ominous note creates an anticipation about the nature of "the kid" which will be resolved only in the last part of the play, and lets us know that the subject of "the kid" is one with which George and Martha are quite familiar and that it is also quite private between them.

As George is about to open the door, he says things that arouse Martha's anger to the point that she screams "SCREW YOU!" just as the door is opened so that it appears that she screams this invective at the newly arrived guests, Nick and Honey. This comment becomes the central metaphor for the rest of the drama. It becomes obvious that Martha invited Nick and Honey because she is physically attracted to Nick and constant allusions will be made about Nick's body which he keeps in good shape. The fact that she yells the comment to Nick conforms with her later attempts to seduce the young man.

Other than the term having sexual meaning, "screw" also carries a connotation of getting to someone or getting even with someone or confusing someone. Each of these meanings also applies to the play. After George has later been humiliated by Martha, he then initiates the game "Getting the Guests" in which he gets even with the guests and also gets them thoroughly confused before Nick understands the final truth about "the kid." Another meaning of screw is to tighten, to twist, to apply pressure or to coerce. George constantly applies pressure to Honey and twists her tipsy memory around to make her corroborate his story about the telegram. Then, of course, the term "to screw up" means to make a mess of things. Martha certainly did this when she revealed the "bit about the kid." In fact, by normal standards, George and Martha's lives have been all screwed up for years. Also, to be "screwed out of" means that one has been taken advantage of or cheated in some way. At one point or another in the play each character is taken advantage of by some other character. And, finally, a screw or a screw ball refers to a very eccentric person. George and Martha's behavior or life style and their imaginary child could certainly be classified as eccentric or unusual behavior. Consequently, the two words hurled at George but hitting Nick and Honey become central to the rest of the drama.

ACT I: Scene ii

Scene ii begins with the entrance of Nick and Honey and ends when Martha takes Honey to the bathroom, leaving George and Nick alone.

With the entrance of Nick and Honey, who have heard Martha scream her invective, "Screw You," Martha, Nick and Honey attempt some sort of diversionary conversations. George constantly shows his superior wit by his witty repartee. When Nick tries to make social conversation by commenting on an original oil painting, George responds that it was by "some Greek with a mustache Martha attacked one night. . . ." Thematically, this comment emphasizes Martha's aggressive nature and suggests her later attempts to seduce young Nick. The discussion shifts to a conversation about drinking, then to the rememberance of the ditty "Who's Afraid of Virginia Woolf" and ends with the discussion of the party at Martha's father's house. All of these interchanges are characterized by some of the wittiest dialogue in modern drama. But the dramatic interest in these witticisms lies in the fact that undoubtably Martha and George have been saying *exactly* the same witty things over and over, year after year to new faculty members. It is not the first time that George has described Martha's drinking habits or the nature of her mind or the basic characteristics of Martha's father's parties. Consequently, we should remember that each comment is somewhat "fed" to the newcomers and that Martha and George are staging a "performance" for the young couple. It is important to establish that this "routine" exists in order to understand later on that the subject of their child has never been mentioned.

Just as Martha and Honey are leaving, George once again reminds Martha: "Just don't shoot your mouth off . . . about . . . you-know-what." This is another ominous warning, and we are further alerted when Martha threatens that she will "talk about any goddamn thing I want to." This now prepares the reader for the fact that when Martha does reveal something about "the kid" that drastic measures will have to be taken.

ACT I: Scene iii

With the departure of Martha and Honey, we begin scene iii with George and Nick who talk of George's "dashed hopes," the "musical beds" among the faculty, of their relative ages and ambitions, and of the differences between history and biology.

The conflict in this scene is between two approaches to life, epitomized by the major difference between history and biology — George accuses Nick of trying to rearrange mankind's "chromozones" (which he mistakes for chromosomes, thus showing his little knowledge about biology) and therefore to adjust the future of mankind, while Nick constantly fails to understand George's classical allusions (he does not know that "Parnassus" is the mountain where the great Greek poets and philosophers were supposed to live after death) and thus reveals that he (Nick) is not concerned with human history, and prefers the scientific approach to a humanistic approach. Early in the scene George sets up intellectual traps for Nick who falls into them; but when George calls for a response to his declension "Good, better, best, bested," Nick refuses to participate any longer in George's *game*. Since the title of the act is "Fun and Games" we are thus exposed to one of the themes basic to the play. Ultimately, as we will see when we learn about the imaginary child, George and Martha's entire marriage has been a type of "fun and games," deception and illusion. Their bantering and hurling of insults throughout this first act is also a type of game. If one were to read Eric Berne's *Games People Play* (1964), one would discover that games can become various types of substitutes for real emotions. The titles of other games played later in the drama include "Humiliate the Host," "Hump the Hostess," "Get the Guest," "Bringing Up Baby," "Peel the Label," "Houseboy," and "Kill the Kid." Each game will be seen to function on its own level. And as with all games, there are certain rules that must be observed. When

Martha violates the rules of their game, George must, at the end of the drama, bring the game to an end and in such a way that the guests will never reveal the existence of the game to anyone.

When Nick refuses to play the game and threatens to leave immediately, George refuses to let him go because, by this time, George is aware that maybe Nick *does* have some ability to play in the various games—that suddenly Nick exhibits some liveliness that wasn't apparent before. Thus by persuading Nick to stay, the games will continue for a while longer. George emphasizes that it is only a game by assuring Nick that Martha and he are not having an argument—instead, they are merely ". . . exercising . . . we're merely walking what's left of our wits." In actual life, this is another key to George and Martha's personal relationship: they enjoy witty repartee and a love/hate relationship that is expressed through their verbal violence. Ultimately it is amazing how much hostility and hatred they can throw at each other only to turn immediately to each other for emotional support.

This scene closes with the allusion to another game—or the same one. When Nick asks George if he has any children, George answers with a juvenile reply: "That's for me to know and you to find out"—a type of retort that is common among young children. The emphasis on child-bearing is carried further when George inquires, in turn, about Nick's plans for a family, preparing us later for the revelation about Honey's alleged pregnancy.

When Nick implies that he might want to settle in this college town, George calls the place "Illyria . . . Penguin Island . . . Gomorrah. . . . You think you're going to be happy here in New Carthage, eh?" These allusions have varying significance. Illyria was the idealized seacoast in Shakespeare's *Twelfth Night; Penguin Island* is both an illusionary and realistic satire on civilization; Gomorrah was the most sinful city in the *Old Testament* and was completely destroyed by God because of the lustfulness of its people; and Carthage was the scene of the greatest of the "unholy love affairs" of ancient times—that of Dido and Aeneas. Thus each is, in some way, a reflection of various aspects of *Who's Afraid of Virginia Woolf.*

ACT I: Scene iv

Scene iv is very short. Honey returns to tell the others that Martha is changing so as to be more comfortable. Honey wants to know more about George and Martha's twenty-one-year-old son, and George is stunned to hear this news and threatens to get even with Martha in some way.

While this scene is very short, it is also a turning point in the drama. George is aware, first, that if Martha is changing clothes, she is changing for the hunt, for the kill, the seduction. As George tells the young couple, "Martha hasn't changed for *me* in years" meaning not that she has not changed her clothes, but her basic life style. Only at the end of the drama will Martha have to face the fact that she must change—she can no longer live as she has.

When George hears that Martha has mentioned their "son," he wheels around "as if struck from behind." His insistence upon hearing it again as though he were *"nailing it down"* (stage directions) indicates clearly that this is the *first* time that the son has been mentioned in front of others. His first reaction is an ominous warning with threatening overtones. The fact that an outsider now knows about this means that George cannot allow them to leave with the knowledge of their imaginary son—that he must keep the guests in his house until he can discover what to do.

ACT I: Scene v

Martha returns in a "most voluptuous" dress and begins to openly admire Nick's body and to discuss it, and at the same time, to ridicule both George's position in the college and his physique. When Martha is about to begin on a boxing story after finding out that Nick was a boxer, George leaves.

Other than the wit involved, this scene mainly shows Martha as an aggressive, seductive female, who is also enjoying playing some type of game. She varies at one moment from baby talk to vituperative language. She cuddles up to George and then throws him off balance with her insults. She belittles his position in the History Department as well as his physical abilities. Then turning from George, she openly admires Nick's fine body and there "is a rapport of some unformed sort established" between them—a rapport filled with double meanings. At this point and for some time to come, Martha has the upper hand over George: it will not be until much later in the drama that George will again gain control of the situation.

ACT I: Scene vi

This very short scene involves Martha's narrating a story about how at the beginning of World War II, her father wanted everyone in good physical condition, so one day when people had boxing gloves on, she put on a pair and accidently knocked George into a huckleberry bush.

The actual boxing scene between George and Martha corresponds to their constant verbal sparring. As with the first act of the drama, Martha wins the first round of the boxing match, but George will be the ultimate victor in the final contest. As Martha relates the story, she tells the young people that "It was funny, but it was awful." This phrase characterizes her attitude about their entire marital relationship.

ACT I: Scenes vii — ix

These two short scenes begin with George continuing with the fun and games. He returns with the fake gun and pretends that he is going to shoot Martha. Since the arguments between George and Martha have been so vituperative and seemingly bitter, Nick and Honey are horrified. (In some productions, the gun explodes with an American flag rather than a Chinese parasol. While the American flag emphasizes rather lamely the underlying parody of American life and values, the Chinese parasol carries through more aptly the idea of the fun and games.) Furthermore, the gun is an obvious sexual symbol which delights Martha's sensuous self. In the same scene, she refers to George as "You . . . prick." At the end of the scene, she delights in using double meanings when she tells Nick that she bets he won't need a fake gun, or any other "props."

When Martha finds out that Nick is not in math but in biology, she continues her vulgar suggestiveness by maintaining that biology is closer "to the *meat* of things."

Scene ix opens with Martha telling Nick as he re-enters: "You're right at the meat of things, baby" a phrase she repeats until George tells her that she is obsessed with it. There is then the discussion, begun earlier in the third scene, concerning the sciences and the humanities. During this scene, as biological matters are discussed and as Martha becomes more and more attracted to young Nick, she increasingly degrades George. In a type of discussion reminiscent of science fiction, George defends the "glorious variety and unpredictability" of the human race against the scientist's idea of creating test-tube babies according to a certain pattern. George, the intellectual humanist, argues for "surprise, the multiplexity" found in natural birth. Nick, the scientist, stands for the creation of a "civilization of men, smooth, blond, and right at the middle-weight limit." George's stand against Nick can also be seen as a defense against all the forces which are threatening the "sanctity" of his home.

As George defends the rights of humans, the subject of his "son" is brought up by Honey. At first, the imaginary son is referred to as an "it" which is quite appropriate. George, however, is the one who insists that Martha tell about their son because she is the one who brought it (him) up. And the subject of the son becomes the *raison d'etre* for the remainder of the play: that is, George must "get the guests" in order to preserve the sanctity of the hearth. The scene ends with George going to get more booze.

ACT I: Scenes x and xi

In George's absence, Martha tells her guests (and thus the audience) how she met and married George. Earlier she had married a young gardener at a finishing school, but her father annulled the marriage immediately. Then she decided to marry someone in the college and "along came George" who in fact returns at this moment "bearing hooch." At first, George goes along with Martha's story, thinking that it concerns their courtship. When he realizes otherwise, he warns her to stop because he now sees that she is leading up to telling about his failures. He reminds her that she has already spilled the beans about their son and now, he says, "if you start in on this other business, I warn you, Martha, it's going to make me angry." Even though he warns her again and again, she continues with the story of his failures.

She tells how it was assumed that George would be groomed to take over her father's place someday. But George wasn't ambitious—in fact he was " . . . a FLOP! A great . . . big . . . fat . . . FLOP!" At this point, George breaks a bottle on the portable bar, but Martha continues even though George is at the breaking point himself. As Martha continues her vicious recounting of George's failures and ineptitudes, he begins to sing "Who's Afraid of Virginia

Woolf" and is joined by the drunken Honey, who becomes sick and rushes down the hall to vomit. Nick and Martha follow her, leaving the crushed and semi-tragic figure of George standing entirely alone. George is at the depth of his existence now with his life laid bare. We have now finished the game of "Humiliating the Host." For the moment Martha has triumphed and George is defeated.

WALPURGISNACHT

ACT II: Scenes i – iii

The subject matter of scenes i – iii concerns George's and Nick's views of their respective wives and other matters. It is briefly interrupted (less than a page) by Martha's appearance to report on the state of Honey's relative sobriety or drunkenness; otherwise, without this brief interruption, this should be considered thematically as one scene.

Act II begins with Nick reporting that Honey is "all right." George then inquires about Martha. In a comic interchange, there is a confusion (deliberate on George's part) as to which wife is being talked about. The confusion begins logically when George asks Nick about the whereabouts of Martha. Nick answers that "she's making coffee" and then in the same sentence says that "She [meaning Honey] gets sick often." George, preoccupied with Martha, takes this opportunity to deliberately misunderstand Nick and therefore puts Nick on the defensive. Because Nick has just witnessed George's humiliation, George wants to make Nick uncomfortable. The hostility between the two men increases as each expresses his antagonism by attacking the other's wife. Nick refers to Martha's and George's abilities to flagellate each other as being very impressive. George retaliates by referring to Honey's tendency to "throw up a lot."

Suddenly there is a startling switch from hostility to confidentiality as the two men begin to reveal things about their respective wives. If we remember, as Nick will later point out, that they have been drinking since 9 P.M. and it is now in the early hours of the morning, then we realize that in such a drunken state, there can easily be a switch from hostility to congenial confidences.

In the course of the conversation, Nick reveals that he married

Honey because she thought she was pregnant. It turned out, however, to have been a hysterical pregnancy: "She blew up and then she went down"; that is, she had all the symptoms of pregnancy without actually being pregnant and while she was in this state, they were married. Later on, however, we discover that it was not a forced marriage — there had been many other factors influencing the marriage; they had known each other since early childhood, it was assumed by both families that they would marry, Honey's father had a great deal of money, and they did care for each other very much.

George then confides in Nick by telling a story about a boy who accidently shot his mother and some time later this boy was in a bar and ordered a "bergin and water," which caused the entire bar to begin laughing and ordering the same. Later the boy was driving a car with "his learner's permit in his pocket" and swerved to "avoid a porcupine and drove straight into a large tree" and killed his father. The boy had to be put into an asylum — "That was thirty years ago."

George's story of the boy who had accidentally shot his mother and then killed his father in an auto accident will be repeated twice again in the drama — it is the subject of George's novel which Martha's father refuses to allow George to publish and it is also the basis for the story of the death of George and Martha's imaginary child. Since the "narrated events" about this boy occurred about thirty years ago (at which time George would have been about sixteen, near the age of the "fictional" boy) and since the same is the subject of his first novel (most first novels are often thinly disguised autobiographies) we can assume that these events possibly happened to George himself. If so, we can use these events to explain George's silence (his refusal to publish), his general withdrawal from life, and his preference for an imaginary child — one who can't kill his parents — to a real child. We could further suggest that George tolerates Martha's disparagement of him because he feels he deserves it.

After the confidential talk, the conversation returns to the two wives. After George has mentioned again Honey's imaginary pregnancy, George casually asserts that "Martha doesn't have pregnancies at all." This statement should alert us (or Nick) that their son is an imaginary one. Yet, continuing in the line of "Fun and Games," George refers to their son as a "bean bag" — a type of object children play with and thus it is an appropriate label for an imaginary child.

After a brief interruption by Martha (scene ii) which includes their hurling obscene French words at each other, George discovers that Nick does have very ambitious plans about "taking over" matters at the university and one way might be for Nick to start sleeping around with certain influential wives. At first, this was part of the "fun and games," but suddenly both George and Nick realize the seriousness of the idea and it frightens Nick more than George. George honestly tries to warn Nick that there is "quicksand here" and that Nick will "be dragged down, just as . . ." but he does not finish his sentence, which implies that George knows that he has been dragged down. Nick refuses to listen and responds with a vicious "UP YOURS!" which prompts George to make an absurd speech about a civilization based on moral principles being reduced to "UP YOURS." After this absurd speech, applauded by Nick, Martha reappears, leading Honey.

ACT II: Scene iv

This scene begins with the entrance of Martha and Honey, continues with the narration by Martha of George's attempts to publish a novel, and then shifts to George's narration which is a description of Honey and Nick's courtship and marriage, presented as though it were the subject of George's new novel. The scene ends when Honey runs off stage to throw up again.

The scene is one of the longest in the drama and is organized around two significant games. The first game is "Humiliate the Host," and the second is "Get the Guests." A third game, "Hump the Hostess," is mentioned but is postponed until a later time. The first game begins with a long discussion in which Martha attacks George and accuses him of causing Honey to throw up. Honey assures them that she has always had a tendency to throw up. Martha again violates her and George's private rules of the game by mentioning their "son." She maintains that "George makes everybody sick. . . ." Then she carelessly mentions how George used to make their son sick. At first, George is again shocked that their son is so openly discussed, but then he plunges into the discussion, using their son as the subject of his wit as he begins to make up stories of how their son was terribly upset because Martha would come in to him with her "kimono flying" and would attempt to corner him with an implied intent to commit incest. Martha retaliates by screaming that she "NEVER CORNERED THE SON OF A BITCH IN MY LIFE!" Clearly, she could not have as he did not exist, but ironically, as she is portrayed, the imaginary child is the son of a verbal bitch.

The first game, "Humiliate the Host," certainly is precipitated by Honey's request for more brandy, followed by George's comment that he used to drink brandy. This comment prompts Martha to remind him that he also used to drink "bergin." The mention of "bergin" then prompts Martha to begin her story of George's unpublished novel.

From George's pleading attempts to get Martha to refrain from telling the story, we can conclude that she has told the story to other people before, especially since Martha twice repeats that George usually tells his side of the story also. At this point George decides that he has to find "some new way to fight" against Martha's destructive impulses.

After Honey suggests dancing, the two couples pair off in a sort of symbolic parody of "partner swapping," and while Martha and Nick are dancing, with all sorts of suggestive body movements, Martha completes her humiliation of her husband by revealing the most personal and intimate details of her husband's failure in life — that is, she riducules his professional ineptitude and his cowardice in the manner in which he yielded to her father's demands that he not publish his book. Her father's ordering George not to publish is the worse type of intellectual censorship and for George to yield to this is extreme intellectual cowardice. George has, however, learned to live with it until this night when Martha violates another of the basic rules of their game — she reveals publicly not only one of their personal failures, but also reveals illusions that they have used to avoid facing their failures.

The humiliation for George is so intense because in his previous conversations with Nick, he has presented himself (or has posed as) a champion of truth and intellectual freedom. Now Martha has exposed her husband as a fraud before a vigorous, handsome young man. Thus, Martha's exposé of all of George's weaknesses and of the lies he tells to cover up his failures so profoundly humiliates him that he physically attacks Martha violently, trying to choke her into silence. Whereas the attack against Martha with the toy pop gun was comic, this attack is no longer comic; it carries with it the true seeds of violence and the possibility of great physical harm. This scene thus becomes a significant turning point in the drama as we see that George *"is hurt, but it is more a profound humiliation than a physical injury."* Martha perceptively recognizes this potential danger and after Nick has stopped the attack, she calls George a "murderer." Thematically, in the next act he will become a murderer as he kills his own son, and may have been a murderer in his past.

Even though George is now at his lowest depths, he quickly recovers and announces that they have successfully completed the game of "Humiliate the Host" and now they must find another game. Since it is not time yet for "Hump the Hostess," George suggests a game of "Get the Guests" in which he proceeds to tell the plot of his second novel—a surprise to Martha. In a thinly disguised allegory, George proceeds to tell the story of Nick and Honey's engagement and marriage with all the appropriate background about Honey's father. At the climax of the story, Honey realizes that this is her story, and she realizes that Nick has *betrayed* the most personal details of their past. This betrayal makes her physically sick and she rushes again from the room.

In narrating the story, George is able to show Nick how it feels to be humiliated by placing Nick in such a position. He also directly exposes Nick as a person who cannot be trusted with a secret, so that the events of this night might not be safe with someone so untrustworthy. By exposing Nick, he is also able to show Martha that her new infatuation is for a person of questionable integrity.

ACT II: Scenes v and vi

In scene v, Nick tells of his resentment about the story George has revealed and threatens to get even with George and then exits to look after Honey. After he is gone, George and Martha argue about the events of the night.

In the conversation between George and Martha, George tells her of his resentment of the humiliating way she has treated him. Martha assumes that George is masochistic enough that he wants to be treated (or humiliated) the way he has been: "YOU CAN STAND IT!! YOU MARRIED ME FOR IT!!" She believes that George needs her to whip him so that he will not have to take any blame for his failures. Although George sees the truth in this, he feels she has gone too far and his future actions will allow him to try to correct this situation. The scene ends with both declaring "total war" against each other.

ACT II: Scenes vii – ix

In scene vii, Nick re-enters to report that Honey is resting on the tiles of the bathroom floor. In scene viii, while George is out getting ice, Martha and Nick continue their sexual flirtation and Martha is the aggressor. George re-enters, notices their actions, and exits again without acknowledging them. He re-enters a moment later singing "Who's Afraid of Virginia Woolf," delivers the ice, and then ignores them, sits in a chair and reads a book about history. This infuriates Martha because she does not know how to react to this new behavior. This scene has not been programmed and she has the sense that she is losing control of the situation. As George ignores them, pretending to be content with his book, Martha becomes "livid" with anger since she is obviously using Nick to make George angry. She then sends Nick to the kitchen to wait.

In scene ix, George's pretended obliviousness to the sex play going on between Nick and Martha causes Martha to threaten that she will indeed go to bed with Nick if George doesn't stop her. Martha's frantic threats such as "I swear to God I'll do it," "I swear to God I'll follow that guy into the kitchen, and then I'll take him upstairs . . ." and "I'll make you regret. . . ." indicate that this is indeed the *first* time that she has ever gone this far. In spite of the fact that Martha has been presented otherwise, this night represents a new departure for George and Martha. It is the first time that their "son" has been mentioned to outsiders, and it is also the first time that Martha has gone so far in seducing another person.

ACT II: Scenes x and xi

In scene x, George is left alone and his reactions reveal his inner emotions. The passage from the book George is reading, Spengler's *Decline of the West*, is appropriate because it deals with "crippling alliances" and "a morality too rigid to accommodate itself. . . ." After a pause, he violently hurls the book at the chimes. If this type of scene (between Martha and Nick) had been a frequent occurrence, George would be accustomed to it. Instead, however, he is hurt and bewildered. His desperation is expressed in his hurling the book.

In scene xi, the chiming awakens Honey who has been dreaming. In telling about her dream, Honey reveals that she does not want children — that she is afraid. George immediately perceives that Honey's headaches, nausea, and "whining" stem from something other than alcohol. The implication is either that she aborted her first pregnancy out of fear of childbirth or currently takes, and will continue, to take birth control pills to prevent the pregnancies that Nick might want or expect her to have. In addition, she remains "childlike" (sucking her thumb, sleeping in a fetal position) to avoid having to face the adult responsibility of pregnancy. In contrast to Martha, the "earth mother" who can't have any children, Honey is the eternal child who refuses to have any children.

When a loud noise ("the crashing of dishes") is heard off stage, George tries to tell Honey what is going on between Martha and Nick, but she only wants to know who *rang* the *chimes*. George puns that the bang, bang of the bells announce the sexual bang, bang of Martha and Nick's affair, but Honey ignores this.

The query about the bells inspires George to conceive of a way to get back at Martha. He convinces Honey that the doorbell was rung by a messenger with the news that his and Martha's son is dead. Since the audience does not yet know that the son is an imaginary one, George's decision to tell Martha that their son is dead would appear to the audience to be an extremely cruel lie — a horrible, sick joke that goes beyond the boundaries of the other *games* that they have been playing.

THE EXORCISM

ACT III: Scene i

In scene i, Martha is alone, and her soliloquy reveals her sense of abandonment and a desire to make up with George. She imagines a scene where they admit that they would do anything for each other. After remembering the game, "Hump the Hostess," she prepares the audience for Nick's failure by repeating "Fat chance . . . Fat chance." She goes on to talk about her father, herself, and George and recognizes the sadness and bitterness that underscores her relationship with them both.

ACT III: Scene ii

In this scene between Nick and Martha, Nick reports that Honey is again lying curled up on the bathroom tiles and is peeling the label off the brandy bottle. This scene ends when George enters with the snapdragons.

The first significant revelation is that, for all of his youthfulness and acclaimed athletic prowess, Nick has been "a flop" in bed. "A flop" is used several times in this scene to emphasize Nick's failure. Even though Nick blames alcohol for his sexual failure in bed, the fact that he has failed causes Martha to look at her own failures and inadequacies and to realize that George is the only person who can fulfill her emotionally and physically. She realizes it is "George who is good to me, and whom I revile; who understands me and whom I push off; who can make me laugh, and I choke it back . . . who keeps learning the games we play as quickly as I can change the rules; who can make me happy and I do not wish to be happy. . . ."

Nick, in his youthful vigor, finds it unbelievable that George can satisfy Martha. Martha, who now calls herself the "Earth Mother," comes to George's defense and relegates Nick to the position of "houseboy," which signals yet another game. In other words, if Nick can't perform in bed, then he can at least be a houseboy. As the doorbell rings, she orders him to answer it. When Nick resists being reduced to the level of a "flunky," Martha hurls at him an insulting remark about his impotence: ". . . Answer the door. There must be something you can do well; or, are you too drunk to do that, too? Can't you get the latch up, either?" Then she reminds Nick of his ambitions and career: "You didn't chase me around the kitchen . . . out of mad, driven passion, did you now? You were thinking a little bit about your career, weren't you? Well, you can just houseboy your way up." Thus, because Nick, like all the men in Martha's life, has disappointed Martha, he is reduced by her to a houseservant.

ACT III: Scene iii

This scene between George, Martha, and Nick concerns the discussion of Nick as "stud" or "houseboy" and ends when George announces there is one more *game* to be played and sends Nick to bring Honey back onto the scene.

This scene corresponds to or parallels the earlier scene in Act I where George "flings open the door" for Nick and Honey. Whereas earlier George (as the houseboy) had opened the door for Nick to the accompaniment of Martha's "Screw You," now Nick opens the door for George yelling "Christ!" Ironically, George appears in the role of a reverse- or Anti-Christ. But instead of bringing the message of an everlasting life and hope as did Christ, George appears with flowers ("Flores; flores para los muertos.") for the dead and he will assume the omnipotent role of declaring their son to be dead. Thus, as Martha's original "Screw You" had become the central metaphor of the play, now George's assuming a Christ-like authority in deciding matters of the life and death of their son brings about the resolution of the drama.

From the audience's viewpoint, George's comic behavior must seem to be both grotesque and in extremely bad taste since the audience knows that George is here to announce the death of their son. All of his horseplay, his falsetto voice in using a line from Tennessee William's *A Streetcar Named Desire* ("Flores; flores para los muertos"), his choice of snapdragons (hardly an appropriate symbol for death), his comic pretense of mistaking Nick for their imaginary son, the derogatory innuendos concerning their child, the mock-childlike bantering and imitation of courtship — all of this buffoonery must seem terribly out of place in view of the recent "death" of their son.

With his entrance, George brings up the main concerns of the drama and more explicitly, the major concern of this act: the idea of "truth and illusion. Who knows the difference?" — a concern which prompts Nick to later utter his most significant line thus far: "Hell, I don't know when you people are lying, or what." Essentially, the discussion centers on whether or not the moon can come up again after it has gone down. This discussion is interspersed with comments about whether or not Nick could get it up with Martha. Is Nick now the "stud," one who could perform in bed — or is he the "houseboy," one who failed to make it in bed? After Martha lies (we, the audience, know from the preceding scene that Nick was a failure in bed) and says that Nick is "not a houseboy," George is now not certain what is truth and what is illusion. He becomes vindictive by throwing snapdragons at Nick and Martha as though they were spears.

As George tells us, the *games* that they play are getting more serious. The *game* of this scene, "Snap The Dragon," carries overtones of viciousness. While this *game* is being played by George, Nick, and Martha, Honey is off stage playing her sick "solo" game of "peel the label."

George's vindictiveness could be interpreted (as it has been by some critics) as a desire to take out his resentment against Martha and Nick because they have "cuckolded" him. However, in terms of the larger structure of the "games people play," George has already conceded to the idea of Martha and Nick's sexual encounter at the end of Act II. But if one is going to play a *game*, certain rules must be followed. Therefore if Nick "made it in the sack" with Martha, then the rules of the game make him a "stud." If he didn't, then he is a "houseboy." What ultimately disturbs George is that "Someone's lying around here; somebody isn't playing the game straight." The audience knows that Martha and Nick are not adhering to the rules of the new game. As George tells Nick: "If you're a houseboy, you can pick up after me; if you're a stud, you can go protect your plow [i.e., Martha]." It is not that George has to know truth from illusion, but the game requires that "we must carry on as though we did." George then announces that there is one more game to play, "Bringing up Baby," and he sends Nick to "fetch" Honey.

ACT III: Scene iv

In this short scene, Martha pleads for no more games, but George has elaborate plans for the next game and the purpose of the scene is to get Martha primed and in a fighting mood: he wants Martha on her "feet and slugging . . . because . . . we're going to play this one to the death." And ironically, the game will end with the "death" of their son.

ACT III: Scene v

This scene, the longest and also the climactic scene, begins with all four characters on stage and ends with the death of the imaginary son. The principal game is "Bringing up Baby" an ironic twist because after he has been brought up the scene will end with the next game – "Kill the Kid."

With the appearance of Nick and Honey, George re-introduces

the concern of the first act (fun and games), and he announces that during the evening that they have gotten "to know each other, and have had fun and games . . . [such as] curl up on the floor . . . peel the label." Honey's game introduces a new metaphor, peeling the label. This is introduced because in peeling the label we get down to the bone and even "when you get down to bone, you haven't got all the way, yet. There's something inside the bone . . . the marrow" [ellipsis Albee's]. This new metaphor (new game) suggests that once we get to the marrow, there can be no more deeper probing; that is, this game will be *the* game that will cut through all illusion and confront one face to face with reality. For George and Martha, who have not faced reality for about twenty years, this will be a supreme test. Whereas earlier Martha seemingly had the "upper hand," now George realizes the necessity of distinguishing between illusion and reality: the only possible solution to their lives and the only solution to their marriage lies in complete honesty. Consequently, whereas earlier George had tried to prevent Martha from bringing up the subject of their son, it is now George who insists that their son (the bouncey boy) be the subject of the next game, "Bringing Up Baby."

Since the audience knows that George is going to announce the death of their son, this "scene-a-faire" is necessary for the audience to see how complete George and Martha's *illusion really is*. That is, the illusion surrounding the birth is necessary so that the audience can see how completely this illusion has occupied George and Martha's lives. The illusion is not a small portion of their lives. Instead, it has occupied their lives to the most minute detail, as illustrated by whether it was an easy birth or whether Martha "labored to give birth." All of the details are carefully worked out between them—the toys, the child's furniture, the color of the eyes and hair, and other details.

Martha, who has never mentioned "the kid" before others, becomes almost transfigured into a Madonna as she becomes so completely immersed in her own illusion of their child. Martha's narration is both moving and convincing as she correlates her "son's" growth to the epitome of everything that is truth, beauty, wisdom, and earthly perfection. The effect of her narration is to evoke from Honey a desire to have a child of her own.

Dramatically speaking, the audience should be constantly aware that George knows that the child does not exist. Yet before he reveals the death of their son, he too becomes, for the last time, caught up in the illusion. In a shift typical of the play, Martha changes from the Madonna-type figure recalling idyllic episodes about her son to a bitter critic of their sordid home life. George argues violently with Martha about whom the child loved more. Then in the form of a duet, Martha continues the narration about the child while George recites Latin phrases from the *Requiem* and *Kyrie Eleison*.

Martha and Honey are ready to put an end to the games, but George has one more surprise for Martha: "It's about sunny-Jim." He then announces the death of their son:

> *George:* Martha . . . *(Long pause)* . . . our son is . . . dead. *(Silence)* He was . . . killed . . . late in the afternoon . . . *(Silence)* *(A tiny chuckle)* on a country road, with his learner's permit in his pocket, he swerved, to avoid a porcupine, and drove straight into a. . . .
>
> *Martha (Rigid fury):* YOU . . . CANNOT . . . DO . . . THAT!
>
> *George:* . . . large tree.

To the astonishment and confusion of both the audience and Nick, Martha repeatedly insists that she will not allow George to "decide these things," and she attempts to physically attack George. Nick pins Martha's arms behind her because he thinks that she is hysterically overcome with grief. While Nick is holding her, George flippantly and triumphantly tells her: "Now listen, Martha; listen carefully. We got a telegram; there was a car accident, and he's dead. POUF! Just like that! Now, how do you like it?"

Martha's response, *(A howl which weakens into a moan)* "NOOOOOOoooooo," is one of the high dramatic points in the drama and has been likened "to that tragic and awful moment of Sophocles's *Oedipus*, when Oedipus discovers he has not only unwittingly killed his own father but has also married his own mother and fathered her children." (See Richard Amacher, *Edward Albee*, p.106.) Martha continues to attack George's presumption that he can make such a decision by himself. The building of the illusion had been a *joint* effort; thus, she feels betrayed that the illusion is suddenly destroyed. Since the illusion had been so completely a part of her life, its destruction is a death-blow as strong as real physical death.

As Martha demands proof of the death and as George becomes more flippant, Nick gradually begins to understand something that is almost too much for him. When George reminds Martha that she knew the rules and has broken them, Nick finally understands that the child has always been an imaginary one. Consequently, of all of the games that have been played during the course of the drama, this is the most involved and elaborate one. Upon further questioning, Nick realizes that George and Martha created this fantasy to compensate for the fact that they could not have any children, and to give themselves the illusion of a normal home life.

George and Martha's imaginary world was complete and resplendant with every detail necessary to the natural birth and growth of a real child, but one essential rule had to be followed. The game had to be completely private between the two—it could never be mentioned to an outsider. As long as it remained a private game there could be all kinds of variations within the framework. Once, however, the child had been mentioned to other people, everything changed. There could be ridicule stemming from public exposure with all sorts of unknown results. But more importantly George recognizes that the illusion has gone on too long, especially now that Martha cannot distinguish illusion from reality, as indicated in her plea:

"I FORGET! Sometimes . . . sometimes when it's night, when it's late, and . . . and everybody else is . . . talking . . . I forget and I . . . want to mention him . . . but I . . . HOLD ON . . . I HOLD ON . . . I hold on . . . but I've wanted to . . . so often . . . oh, George, you've *pushed* it . . . there was no need . . . there was no need for this. I *men*tioned him . . . all right . . . but you didn't have to push it over the EDGE. You didn't have to . . . kill him."

Also, George wants revenge, and he knows that the only way he can regain the upper hand in their relationship is to destroy Martha's belief in her most precious illusion. However, it is too simple to dismiss his motive as revenge alone. He has recognized the danger in believing in one's lies and it becomes necessary for George to kill the illusion to prevent Martha from becoming completely enslaved by her own fantasies.

George has penetrated past the bone and into the marrow. He has performed the complete exorcism and we must remember that an exorcism is performed for the benefit of the bedeviled— in this case, Martha.

In this final, brief but very moving scene between George and Martha, usually played in a very subdued, low-keyed manner, Martha is still hesitant to accept the death of their imaginary son. Even George falters for a moment when he says: "It will be better . . . maybe." George realizes that they have played with the imaginary child far too long, but he too seems to be afraid of facing reality. When Martha says "I don't suppose, maybe we could. . . ." the implication is that maybe they could find a new type of game for their escapism, but George, while fearful, will not agree.

Consequently, the two characters have divested themselves of their illusions and will now have to face reality completely alone. They are weakened, chastised, and subdued by the events of the evening, and they are now two very frightened and pitiable characters, but they are also two human beings who are communicating with each other with honesty and without illusion.

THE SIGNIFICANCE OR IMPLICATIONS OF THE TITLES OF THE ACTS

Most dramatists do not give titles to the individual acts within a drama. When we encounter a drama in which each act has an individual title, we must consider whether or not the dramatist is making a further statement about the nature of his drama. In *Who's Afraid of Virginia Woolf?* the titles of each of the three acts seem to reinforce the content of each act and also to call attention to some of the central motifs in the play itself.

Act I of any drama introduces the characters, themes, subjects, and ideas that will be prominent both in the first act and throughout the drama. The title of Act I, "Fun and Games," suggests part of the theme of the entire drama—George and Martha's complex game of avoiding reality and creating illusions. Therefore, the title of the first act introduces the use of games as a controlling idea for not only the first act but also for the entire drama with the last game, "Killing the Kid," being the game that also ends the drama.

Even though it is not the first use of a game, the first mention of the word "game" comes from Nick. In fact, perhaps Nick's most astute perception of the entire night occurs immediately after his and Honey's arrival. After being "joshed" about the oil painting, and after being trapped in a semantic exchange about why Nick entered the teaching profession, George asks Nick if he likes the verb declension "Good, better, best, bested." Nick perceptively responds: ". . . what do you want me to say? Do you want me to say it's funny, so you can contradict me and say it's sad? Or do you want me to say it's sad so you can turn around and say no, it's funny. You can play that damn little game any way you want to, you know!" The use of the word *game* calls our attention to the concept of games in the play. In the game of "Good, better, best, bested" Nick realizes that the game is one in which one person manipulates another person. However, teasing, criticizing, ridiculing and humiliating another person is a one-sided game, and after a point, there is a revolt. Nick revolted early against George's teasing and toying with him. George will also later revolt against his own humiliation at the hands of Martha. In a later scene, Nick, in a moment of confusion, tells George and Martha that he can't tell any more when they are playing games and when they are serious. Because of this, it is a long while before Nick "sees through the game" and realizes that George and Martha's child is imaginary. Thus in one way or another, most of the behavior of the evening can be classified as a game whether names and rules for the games are established or not.

Implicit also in the term *game* is the idea that a game *must* have a set of rules. When the rules are violated, then the game takes on other characteristics. George and Martha's life together has been one in which they have consistently played games, but the rules have often been changed. Martha's great reliance on George is that he "keeps learning the games we play as quickly as I can change the rules." Until this night, their game about their kid has been one in which there was only *one* rule—that is, that the entire game must remain completely private between them. Between themselves, they have often changed the rules (was it an easy delivery or a difficult delivery? Were his eyes blue, grey, or green with brown specks?), but the rule of privacy has never been violated until now. Martha's violation of this rule, then, affects the remainder of the drama.

In addition to the above mentioned types of games, the following types of games illustrate how completely Albee has used the concept of "game-playing" as a controlling metaphor of his play.

1. The play opens with a guessing game in which Martha tries to get George to identify a line from a movie they have seen. Variations of guessing games or identification games are found in every echelon of American society from television to academic surroundings.

2. The early announcement of a party implies fun and games since a party is a type of game, especially since Martha screams with childish delight "party, party" with the doorbell chimes.

3. The use of the nursery rhyme or game of "Who's Afraid of the Big Bad Wolf" is first mentioned by George and Martha, mentioned again by Martha to Nick and Honey and then is used to close the act as a raucous duet by George and Honey amid crashing violence. The game is emphasized as a central motif throughout the first act and, of course, the drama itself closes with George softly crooning "Who's Afraid of Virginia Woolf?" to Martha.

4. It is a type of game when George who has been forced to play the role of houseboy has so manipulated Martha that as he opens the door she screams "Screw You" toward Nick and Honey. The many attempts to "screw" one another in one way or another become a type of a game.

5. Fun and games are again the subject of conversation when each recalls the party at Martha's father's house where Nick and Honey "certainly had fun."

6. The incessant interplay or demonstration of wit, whether between Nick and George or between George and Martha pervades the entire act. The game of guessing who painted Martha's picture, or the game of "good, better, best, bested" are word games that are basic to the human personality. In the declension game, as with other games, the game itself implies other things since George himself has been somewhat "bested" by life and certainly by Martha. The various uses of wit throughout the act and especially the unintentionally comic comments by Honey continue throughout the act.

7. Throughout the act, from George's first warning Martha not to "start on the bit about the kid," George and Martha's most intimate and private game — that of their imaginary son — is significantly hinted at and becomes the central idea of the play. For example, when Nick asks George if they have any children, George answers as would a child in fun and games: "That's for me to know and you to find out."

8. The faculty sport "Musical Beds" is a satiric take-off on the

old parlor game "Musical Chairs" and, as the name implies, becomes an adult game by way of the sexual allusions.

9. There are also frequent references to various types of sporting games or sporting events such as handball or football, but more importantly, there is Martha's narration of the boxing contest between her and George and much of the entire act can be viewed as a verbal sparring match between George and Martha with Martha being the victor by the end of the first act.

10. George's trick with the toy pop gun which shoots out a Chinese parasol is a fun type of party game. It fits in with George's earlier comment when he finds out that Martha has invited someone over, in that Martha is always "springing things on me." The surprise of the pop gun, then, is George's "springing something" on Martha.

11. Act I also introduces the various imaginative, alliteratively named games that will be played — "Humiliate the Host," "Hump the Hostess," "Bringing up Baby," "Get the Guest," "The Bouncey Boy," and "Kill the Kid." Later on, other games such as "Snap the Dragon" and "Peel the Label" will also be played.

12. Early in the act when Nick threatens to leave because he fears that he has intruded upon a private family argument, George tells him it's all a game — that we are "merely . . . exercising . . . we're merely walking what's left of our wits."

13. When Martha changes her clothes, it is so that she can make a deliberate play for Nick. As George points out, Martha hasn't changed for him for years, so her actions must have significance in that she "plays" on Nick's ambitions.

14. The entire first act and the entire drama "plays" before an audience as though it was one gigantic game in which no one really knows the rules.

The titles of the second and third acts make a rather direct comment on the action of each act. The title of Act II, "Walpurgisnacht," refers to the night of April 30 which is the time of the annual gathering of the witches and other spirits at the top of Brocken in the Harz Mountains located in Southern Central Germany. It is sometimes referred to as the Witches' Sabbath. During this night, witches and other demons dance, sing, drink, and become involved in all sorts of orgies. This is a night where any type of behavior can be found among the participants, and in literature, or in general language, the term "Walpurgis Night" has come to refer to any situation which possesses a nightmarish quality or which becomes wild and orgiastic. Thus, in Act II, as Honey proceeds to get extremely drunk, the others, especially Martha and Nick, dance in an obvious sensual, semi-orgastic manner. The scene ends in a bizarre manner — a fifty-two-year-old woman takes a twenty-eight-year-old man upstairs for a seduction while her husband quietly reads a book with full knowledge of what is happening upstairs.

In Act III, "The Exorcism," we see the meaning of the term "exorcism" being applied to Martha. During the course of the act George eerily recites the *Kyrie Elieson* and uses incantations, adjurations, and other necessary devices in order to free Martha of the illusion that their "child" exists and to bring her back to a world free of fantasy.

CHARACTER ANALYSES

GEORGE

At the opening of the play, George is seen as Martha's "house boy" — someone who will open the door, mix her a drink, listen to her tirades and be her companion and her "doormat." During the years since George has taught at the college, he has apparently made no effort to take over and run things. Instead, he has been seemingly content with his life as it is. In fact, at one point Martha tells him that he "married her for it" — that is, to be treated exactly as she treats him.

The night depicted in the play is a crucial night for George. Even though there are numerous indications that these types of late parties have occurred for many years and even though the witty dialogue and sarcastic things that are said indicate a highly developed wit, yet this night is the climax of George's life. Because of the events of this night and after it is over, George (and Martha) will have to develop a different type of existence.

The exact nature of George's background is either conjectured or unknown. If we assume that the novel he wrote (if indeed, he did write one) was based on biographical fact, then George's earlier life could have been bizarre — that is, he could have been the young boy who "killed his mother with a shotgun" and then later, while driving along a country road with "a learner's permit in his pocket and his father on the front seat to his right, he swerved the car to avoid a porcupine and drove straight into a large tree." George told Nick the story of the boy as though it were a remembrance, and said that it took place thirty years earlier. Since George is forty-six years old, this could be evidence that points to George as the subject of the story, and it would suggest why George has never attempted to force himself into the forefront of activity.

Later, Martha reveals that George wrote a novel with the same plot, and she goes on to make a rhyme suggesting that George used his own past as the basis of his novel. She also says that George told her father that the events described in the book really happened to George. Since Martha also refers to George's having at one time liked "bergin," there is convincing evidence for assuming that George and the boy in the story are one and the same.

Knowing this may shed some light on George's preference for the imaginary child over a real one. Certainly an imaginary child could never actually kill his own father, as George possibly did.

For years, George has gone along with and contributed to the myth that they have a child. This illusion is so completely developed between them that every aspect of the child's birth (from labor pains to the color of the eyes) can be described in detail. But until this crucial night, they have never told any outside person about their "kid." In the first act, George warns Martha three times "Just don't start in on the bit about the kid." At this point, George still sees the need of concealing their illusion—he is fully aware of the ridicule they would be subjected to. And since their life is bizarre enough as it is, George realizes the necessity of keeping their illusions to themselves.

After George has been thoroughly humiliated by Martha and after he is fully aware that Martha has talked about the "kid," he realizes that Martha is losing touch with reality, and that for their protection from public ridicule and, more importantly, to keep Martha from living completely in a world of fantasy, he must "kill" the child. On a superficial level, it would at first seem that he kills the child to get revenge on Martha for the humiliation she has subjected him to. If this were true, we would dismiss George as a petty, spiteful, revengeful person of no consequence. Instead, it is his attachment to Martha which prompts him to "kill" the child because he sees the necessity of destroying the illusions and fantasies which are controlling both of their lives and is about to destroy Martha's.

In the final scene, George realizes that they can't continue with their illusion, and even though he is also apprehensive, he realizes that they must attempt to create a new life for themselves. For George and as well for Martha, this is to be a frightening new experience.

MARTHA

From the opening of the play until the final scenes and particularly until George "kills" their son, Martha dominates the action. Elizabeth Taylor, playing the role of Martha in the movie version of the play, won an Academy Award for her performance. This role is one of the choice parts for an actress, demanding a great deal of versatility and ability.

As the daughter of the president of the college, Martha automatically carries a certain amount of clout which accounts for the arrival of the young guests at such a late hour.

Basically Martha is a domineering, forceful and earthy person. She best characterizes herself, when she refers to herself as an "earth mother" who constantly wants to get at "the meat of the matter." She freely sprinkles her speeches with curse words and obscene words, remarks, and gestures. She openly makes known her sexual attraction toward the youthful Nick and delights in the concept of the game "Hump the Hostess." During the course of drama, Martha virtually ignores the presence of Honey.

Martha delights in letting people know that George is a "flop" — that he has not taken over the history department as she had expected (in fact, Martha uses the word *flop* to also apply to Nick when he can't make it in bed). Martha uses the fact that George has not lived up to her expectations as a reason to demean him. She also believes that George desires her to castigate him — that he married her partly for that reason.

Martha knows that she can push George only so far, and she recognizes that George is the only person who can satisfy her physically and emotionally. Even though she has enjoyed the humor of "Hump the Hostess" and her assumed reputation of sexual liberation, it is ultimately seen that Martha has not been promiscuous (if for no other reason than because the daughter of the president of the university should not be so indiscreet). In the narration of the birth and life of their child, Martha takes on an indulgent, maternal aspect that is almost "Madonna-like." We come to understand that she needs the illusion of being a mother. The illusion is so real now that she has revealed the "existence" of their child for the first time. In other words, she has allowed the world of illusion to intrude upon the world of reality.

Therefore, when George "Kills the Kid," Martha is truly frightened of the consequences, and she expresses her fear in terms of the nursery rhyme — she is afraid of the big bad wolf, or in other words, she is afraid of facing reality.

The abrasiveness, the domineering nature, and the strength which Martha had earlier demonstrated has now left her and we see her at the end of the drama as a person who needs pity and compassion.

NICK

To George, Nick represents the "new wave of the future." It is significant that he is teaching biology for two reasons. First as a biologist, he becomes a representative of the scientists who experiment with chromosomes, genes, and by extension, our future. George accuses him of trying to readjust our "chromozones." Nick is the perfect foil for George because they represent the opposite extremes in scholarship — George, history, the past, and Nick, biology, the future. Second, it is emphasized that Nick is in good physical condition. This, coupled with Nick's field, concerned as it is with the physical, symbolizes his role in the play and Martha's physical attraction to him. She certainly does not invite him over because of his mental attributes.

Nick is best characterized by his ambitions. While it is true that he is genuinely fond of his wife (he and Honey had known each other since childhood and were expected to marry), he did marry her partly because of her money, which would abet his ambitions. Nick's ambition is attested to by the fact that he even bothers to come to George and Martha's after-the-party party. As Martha points out later, Nick is fully aware that Martha is the daughter of the president of the university, and he certainly did not chase her around the kitchen because of mad passionate desire.

Nick is, therefore, trapped by the events of the evening. He wants to please but he finds it awkward to stay and watch two middle-aged people verbally cutting each other to pieces. He also wants to please (or satisfy) Martha sexually, but in agreeing to drink with the two of them, he has unwittingly rendered himself sexually impotent.

Nick is blind to the fact that his wife is frightened to have children. Basically, he treats her as a child. He is constantly concerned about the nature of George's language in front of Honey (ironically, he doesn't make any protestations about Martha's equally strong language). And whereas he will openly flirt with Martha and dance sensually with her, he is offended if George makes even the slightest reference to Honey's sexuality.

Nick, while slow in recognizing George and Martha's child as being a product of the imagination, does finally realize their plight, and, as a result, is horrified by the realization. He does not possess the perception to understand why George and Martha have created the child; instead, he is totally perplexed by the revelation. Ultimately, Nick, then, is seen as a male conformist who is caught up in a non-conformist atmosphere (George and Martha's house and party) where even his physical attributes fail him and thus, he finds himself in an inferior position with which he cannot cope.

HONEY

From the viewpoint of the actress playing the role, Honey is a choice part. The role has received accolades from the audiences of both theater and film. Sandy Dennis won an Academy Award as the best supporting actress for her performance of Honey in the film version of the drama.

We know very little about Honey. We hear from Nick that her father was some type of minister (or evangelist) who amassed a considerable amount of money. We know that Honey and Nick were childhood "sweethearts" and that she apparently became pregnant before marriage. Whether or not it was a hysterical pregnancy which "went away" after her marriage or a real pregnancy which she had aborted, we can never be sure. George, in one scene, assumes that she aborted her pregnancy and that she has either continued to have abortions or else continually takes some type of birth control pill. From her own comments, we know that she is terribly afraid to have children because she is exceptionally afraid of the pain involved in childbirth.

Honey is either fey, childlike or drunk in almost every scene. In view of the fact that she refuses to face the reality of childbearing, it therefore follows that her actions are those of an adult child, and her husband, Nick, will often treat her as one by trying to protect her from certain language, from sexual references and by constantly overseeing her actions. Her childlikeness is further emphasized by her habit of gurgling, being obtuse to the reality of the situation around her and, ultimately, by curling up in a fetal position when she is drunk and peeling the labels off liquor bottles.

As a result of the activities of the night, Honey has apparently undergone some sort of change. Whether or not it is a permanent catharsis or a temporary change, we do not know. We are aware however, that Honey suddenly changes her mind and wants to have children. "I want a child," she cries as they leave. This is a complete change from the Honey who told George about an hour earlier that she wanted no children.

In the final analysis, we cannot be sure how much of the events of the evening Honey is aware of. Whereas Nick comes to a complete recognition that George and Martha have been talking about an imaginary child, we cannot be certain that Honey has understood this. Finally, we realize that Honey has stood outside the main stream of the action for the entire evening, inhabiting, essentially, her own private world of brandy, peeling labels, and solo dancing.

REVIEW QUESTIONS

1. The play takes place between 2 A.M. and dawn. Is the time significant, then, in terms of the events of the night?

2. How can you account for the lack of interaction between Martha and Honey?

3. Do you think most relationships are characterized by various types of game-playing? Why or Why not? Are games always harmful?

4. What are the elements of a tragedy? Does this play qualify as a tragic drama?

5. Do you believe that personalities are "inherent" or that "events shape people"? Discuss each character in terms of how each is portrayed and whether or not there are reasons for each character's present situation.

6. What does Honey learn from her exposure to George and Martha?

7. Do you approve of Nick's ambition?

8. What does the title of the play mean?

SELECTED BIBLIOGRAPHY

Albee's Major Works

The Zoo Story, The Death of Bessie Smith, The Sandbox, and Three Plays. New York: Coward-McCann, 1960.

The American Dream. New York: Coward-McCann, 1961.

The American Dream; The Death of Bessie Smith; Fam and Yam. New York: Dramatists' Play Service, 1962.

Who's Afraid of Virginia Woolf? New York: Atheneum, 1962.

Who's Afraid of Virginia Woolf? New York: Pocket Books, 1963-64.

The Play "The Ballad of the Sad Cafe": *Carson McCullers' Novella Adapted to the Stage*. Boston: Houghton Mifflin, 1963, and New York: Atheneum, 1963.

Tiny Alice. New York: Atheneum, 1965.

Malcolm. New York: Atheneum, 1966.

A Delicate Balance. New York: Atheneum, 1966.

Everything in the Garden. New York: Atheneum, 1968.

Box and *Quotations from Chairman Mao Tse-Tung*. New York, Atheneum, 1969.

CRITICISM

Amacher, Richard E. *Edward Albee*. New York: Twayne Publishers, 1969.

Amacher, Richard E. and Margaret Rule, eds. *Edward Albee at Home and Abroad: a Bibliography, 1958 – June 1968*. New York: AMS Press, 1970.

Berne, Eric. *Games People Play*. New York: Grove Press. 1964.

Bigsby, C.W. E. *Albee*. Edinburgh: Oliver and Boyd, 1969.

Diehl, Digby. "Edward Albee Interviewed," *Transatlantic Review* 13 (Summer 1963): 57-72.

Flasch, Joy. "Games People Play in *Who's Afraid of Virginia Woolf?" Modern Drama* 10 (1967): 280-88.

Harris, Wendell V. "Morality, Absurdity, And Albee," *Southwest Review* 49 (Summer 1964): 249-56.

McDonald, Daniel. "Truth and Illusion in *Who's Afraid of Virginia Woolf?" Renascence* 17 (1964): 63-69.

Meyer, Ruth. "Language: Truth and Illusion in *Who's Afraid of Virginia Woolf?" Education Theatre Journal* 20 (1968): 60-69.

Paul, Louis. "A Game Analysis of Albee's *Who's Afraid of Virginia Woolf?"* The Core of Grief." *Literature and Psychology* 17 (1967): 47-51.

Roy, Emil. *"Who's Afraid of Virginia Woolf?* and the Tradition," *Bucknell Review* 3, i (1965): 27-36.